Down to a Science

ROD PETURSON

Editorial Board
David Booth • Joan Green • Jack Booth

STECK-VAUGHN
⊘ Harcourt Achieve

www.HarcourtAchieve.com

10801 N. Mopac Expressway
Building # 3
Austin, TX 78759
1.800.531.5015

Steck-Vaughn is a trademark of Harcourt Achieve Inc. registered in the
United States of America and/or other jurisdictions. All inquiries should
be mailed to Harcourt Achieve Inc., P.O. Box 27010, Austin, TX 78755.

Ru'bicon © 2006 Rubicon Publishing Inc.

www.rubiconpublishing.com

Project Editors: Miriam Bardswich, Kim Koh
Editorial Assistant: Lori McNeelands
Art/Creative Director: Jennifer Drew-Tremblay
Assistant Art Director: Jen Harvey
Designer: Jeanette Debusschere

6 7 8 9 10   5 4 3 2 1

Down to a Science
ISBN 1-41902-390-X

CONTENTS

Examine ...

Experiment ...

Create ...

Find out ...

Invent ...

Discover ...

Observe ...

Record ...

PINCH, SQUEEZE, and ROLL

warm up

Sometimes titles are designed to make you curious so that you want to read more. Think about this title. What things do you pinch, squeeze, and roll?

When he was a young man, Joe McVicker went to work at his dad's chemical company.

One day in 1956, his sister-in-law complained about the modeling clay her students were using in her kindergarten class. It was very hard to roll and it left oily stains on the children's clothing and papers.

Joe gave her some wallpaper cleaner sold by his company. It was non-toxic and wouldn't hurt the children if they happened to put it in their mouths.

The children loved this new modeling material. Soon, other teachers were asking for the wallpaper cleaner for their own students to use.

Joe saw an opportunity. He started his own company called Rainbow Crafts. He sold his new modeling clay, which he called "Play-Doh®," to stores and schools everywhere.

Over two billion cans of Play-Doh® have been sold since then. To this day, the exact recipe is still a closely guarded secret.

non-toxic: *not poisonous for people or animals*

wrap up

Now that you have read the story, what do you think the title was describing? Suggest a different title for the story.

WEB CONNECTIONS

Using the Internet, research the invention story for another toy. Using your findings, write a short article about the toy. Give it a catchy title.

Have you ever wondered where some of the things that you use at home and at school came from?

Creating Crayons

warm up

Think of all of the colors that can be found in a box of crayons. Make a list of the colors.

Over 100 years ago, children did not have crayons for drawing. They used chalk on slate boards, but their pictures would smudge. And if they wanted to draw another picture, they had to erase the first picture.

In 1903, two inventors decided to do something about this problem. Edwin Binney and C. Harold Smith mixed wax, oil, and color to make a new kind of drawing tool, the crayon. They called their crayons "Crayola," which means "oily chalk."

The first box of crayons had eight colors: black, blue, brown, green, orange, red, yellow, and violet. Today, you can find colors with names like dandelion, razzle dazzle rose, laser lemon, or tickle me pink.

CHECKPOINT
Guess the colors of these crayons by their names.

And after making over 100 billion crayons, the company continues to come up with new and exciting colors.

wrap up

1. Imagine that you are creating a new crayon color. What will it look like? What will you call your new color?

2. Many different coloring tools have been invented since Crayola. With a partner, find out about another coloring tool and write a short report on it.

STRANGE CREATURES

SOMETIMES THE STORIES THAT PEOPLE TELL ABOUT MONSTERS HAVE SOME TRUTH IN THEM.

warm up

With a group of friends, talk about the strangest animal that you have ever seen or read about.

A long time ago, people told stories about the strange animals that lived in faraway places. One person would tell another and that person would tell yet another. As the story was repeated, the animal they were describing usually grew stranger and stranger.

Hundreds of years ago, people found the bones, teeth, and what they thought were horns, of a giant creature. Early drawings of this creature show an animal with a long body and wings. When this creature was shown in the water, they called it a "sea serpent." When this creature was shown on land or in the air, they called it a "dragon."

What was this creature? If you guessed a dinosaur, you're right.

About 500 years ago, people living in Greece found the large skull of a creature with one giant eye in the middle of its forehead. They told scary stories about this monster and called it "Cyclops."

It's hard to believe the Greeks were describing an elephant. The elephant has a large opening where its trunk is attached to its head. The Greeks thought the opening in the skull was for a giant eye.

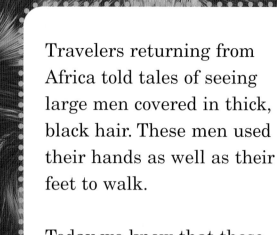

Travelers returning from Africa told tales of seeing large men covered in thick, black hair. These men used their hands as well as their feet to walk.

Today we know that these hairy men aren't men at all — they're gorillas.

FYI

Strange and unknown creatures are still being found today. In 1976, a boat was pulling up its anchor from deep in the ocean near Hawaii. Suddenly the sailors realized that a giant shark over 16.5 feet long was tangled in the lines. This animal, with its huge mouth full of tiny teeth, had never before been discovered.

wrap up

1. Think about a strange-looking animal that is alive today. Write a short description of the animal as if you were seeing it for the very first time. Ask a partner to guess which animal you described.

2. Sometimes early storytellers mixed up the body parts of real animals to create monsters. Dragons had the wings of a bat and the tail of a snake. Draw a picture of an animal that has the parts of other animals. Label the parts.

Megamouth shark—© Bruce Rasner/SeaPics.com

Kangooroo, Kangooroo

Have you ever wondered where the names that we call animals come from? Some animal names came about in pretty weird ways.

warm up

In a group, brainstorm a few animals whose names describe how they sound, look, behave, or move (e.g. a hummingbird or a flying squirrel).

This is the story about how one animal got its name. Some people believe that this story is true. Others argue that it is just an interesting story that has been told by people for a long time.

In 1770, an English explorer by the name of James Cook was sailing around the world in search of new land. Along with the sailors and soldiers on his ship, Captain Cook brought a naturalist whose job was to draw pictures of the wonderful new birds, plants, and animals they would see along the way.

CHECKPOINT

Remember — there were no cameras in those days.

When Captain Cook and his crew landed in what we now call Australia, they went ashore and found a native person, or Aborigine, to guide them in this new land.

FYI

A kangaroo is a marsupial. It has a pouch in which it carries its babies, called "Joeys."

The explorers saw many strange animals. There were the emu, large birds that stood as tall as human beings but could not fly. There were platypuses, small, fur-covered animals that had bills and webbed feet like ducks.

Captain Cook and his men crossed over a mountainous area and found themselves on a large, grassy plain.

There they saw tall, red, and gray animals with large back legs and long, thick tails. The animals hopped long distances with their strong legs. They moved at a great speed.

An excited Captain Cook turned to the naturalist and shouted, "Quick, draw a picture of this strange creature so that we can show people what it looks like."

He then turned to the native guide who was with him and asked, "What do you call this creature?"

CHECKPOINT

Notice the spelling of this word. Read on to find out what it means.

The guide replied, "Kangooroo, kangooroo."

"Write that down with your picture," Captain Cook told the naturalist. "The natives call this animal a kangooroo."

Later, after Captain Cook and his men had traveled back to their ship, the native guide returned to his village.

naturalist: *person who studies plants and animals*

"Where did you go?" the people in the village asked.

"We traveled a long way. Far past where our people have ever gone," he answered.

"What did you see?" they asked him.

"Well, when we were in a grassy area, we saw these strange creatures that hopped along the ground. Captain Cook told one of the men with him to draw a picture of the animal. Then he asked me what the animal was called."

"What did you say?" the people asked.

"I told him — 'I don't know. I don't know.' "

CHECKPOINT

Notice the single quotation marks within the double quotation marks. What does this mean?

wrap up

1. Who spoke the last line in the story? How did you know?

2. Turn this story into a short skit. Decide who will play the role of Captain Cook, the naturalist, and the native guide. Practice your skit and then present it to the class.

INVENTING

warm up

If you could invent a fruit or vegetable, what would it taste and look like? Share ideas in a group.

When we think about inventions, we don't usually think about plants. In fact, some of the fruits and vegetables that we buy in our supermarkets today were actually "invented" by scientists.

CHECKPOINT

"Grafting" is often used with plants. Can you guess what the word means?

GRAFTING
The McIntosh Apple

Over 200 years ago, a Scottish farmer, John McIntosh moved to an area called Dundas County in Ontario, Canada. As he was clearing the land for planting, John discovered some apple trees growing in the brush. He dug up these trees and moved them to a small garden near his cabin.

PLANTS

After some time, one of the trees produced delicious red apples. Word about the apples spread. Before long, people from all around the area came to John's farm to get some of the apples. He soon realized that he could make money by selling trees just like this one.

John tried planting the seeds from the apples, but it didn't work. The trees that grew from the seeds produced sour apples, not anything like the ones from his special tree.

After many experiments, John finally found a way to reproduce his tree. He cut off a branch from the special tree. Then he cut a notch into another small apple tree, and attached the branch from the special tree to it. The attached branch grew and produced the same sweet tasting fruit!

CHECKPOINT

Notice what John did to produce the same sweet tasting fruit.

reproduce: *copy*
notch: *y-shaped cut*

Using this method, called "grafting," John McIntosh produced and sold hundreds of new trees. These trees became known as McIntosh apple trees.

The original McIntosh tree produced sweet, red apples for over 100 years until it finally died in 1910. Today, trees grown from the branches of that original apple tree still produce the McIntosh apples that we find in our grocery stores.

CROSSING

CHECKPOINT

Think about why "crossing" is a good word to describe this process.

Botanists sometimes cross (join together) one kind of fruit or vegetable with another to create something new. Usually they cross one kind of fruit or vegetable with a different variety of the same fruit or vegetable. That is how we have such a wonderful variety of apples, oranges, pears, tomatoes, and other produce in the grocery store.

Plucot

Botanists mixed a plum and an apricot together to make a new kind of fruit — the plucot. Plucots have a smooth outside skin, like a plum, and they are pink on the inside. They taste very sweet.

Aprium

Apriums are a mixture of plums and apricots. The skin of the aprium is fuzzy, just like its apricot parent. This sweet new fruit is a bit bigger than a plucot.

Botanists: *experts who study plant life*
produce: *fresh fruits and vegetables*

SHAPING
How Would You Like It? Square? Round?

For years, botanists have worked to improve fruits and vegetables by changing their shapes and sizes. They produced tiny ears of corn that fit into salads. They grew all kinds of tomatoes, from the little cherry tomato to the giant beefsteak variety.

In England, a new kind of carrot has shown up in supermarkets. These carrots still taste the same, but instead of being long and thin, they are small and round — just the right size for a lunchbox.

In Japan, people have trouble storing big, round watermelons in their small refrigerators. So, the clever Japanese farmers found a way to grow small, square watermelons! The square watermelons stack nicely on the supermarket shelves and in a refrigerator. They take up far less room than the watermelons we are used to seeing, and they taste just as good.

How did the farmers grow square watermelons? Well, it really isn't as hard as you might think.

When the tiny fruit first starts to grow on the vine, farmers place the new watermelon into a square, glass box. The square boxes are just the right size to fit into a refrigerator. As the watermelon grows, it takes the shape of the square box. At just the right time, when the watermelon is ripe, the farmer pops it out of the box — a perfect cube!

Apple/hands–Ablestock; plucot, aprium–istockphoto; Watermelons/os49084/os38061–Getty Images/Photodisc

CHECKPOINT

When you combine two different words, you make a compound word. Find some examples of compound words on this page.

CHECKPOINT

Do you think that a square watermelon would be easier to cut and eat? Why?

wrap up

With a partner, think of two kinds of fruits or vegetables that you could mix to create a better version. Give your new fruit/ vegetable a name. Describe how it tastes and looks. See if your classmates can guess which fruits or vegetables you crossed.

SUPER Inventor

George Washington Carver was born in 1864 in the state of Missouri. He was raised on a farm by his adopted parents. From an early age, George was fascinated by the crops that grew in the area. When he grew older, George began experimenting with plants. He invented many products that we still use today — bleach, buttermilk, chili sauce, instant coffee, mayonnaise, shaving cream, talcum powder, and over 300 uses for peanuts (including peanut butter). Thanks George!

CHECKPOINT

How important are these products to you and why?

wrap up

1. In a small group, find out more about George Washington Carver. Create a collage that shows 20 of his inventions.

2. Do a search! How many of the 300 uses for peanuts can you find?

Igloos are built from blocks of ice. Do you think it is possible to stay warm inside? Discuss with a friend.

The Perfect Igloo

Nestor's Dock

by Tom LaBaff

Hmmm—in search of the perfect igloo.

Well, Nestor, it's nice and, um, white. This would be a good place to spend the night if you wanted to FREEZE TO DEATH.

Well done, Stilts, these thick walls are great for insulation, but what's with the skylight?

It was stuffy in there. I needed to open it up a little.

Great. So in the morning, when you're frozen solid, we can use you as a snowboard.

21

Every winter, not too far from Quebec City, Canada, the Ice Hotel welcomes visitors from all over the world. The walls of this hotel are built from thick blocks of ice. These walls protect visitors from the wind and help keep the inside a lot warmer than you think.

This idea isn't exactly new. The Inuit people of Alaska and northern Canada used to live in dwellings built of snow and ice, called igloos. The igloos protect the Inuit from the cold weather.

Can an igloo keep people warm when it's made of snow and ice? Believe it or not — it can. In fact, it can become so warm inside an igloo that the walls need to be lined with animal skins to stop the snow and ice from melting.

Here are some reasons that an igloo can be so warm:
1. Small spaces take less time to heat.
2. The entrance is a small opening and is protected from the wind.
3. A burning stove and heat from the human body provide warmth inside the igloo.

wrap up

1. Is the igloo in this story a "perfect" igloo? Explain your answer to a friend.

2. Imagine you are Nestor. Write a journal entry to describe your night inside the igloo.

Ask an Expert

Who is the first person you always
go to when you have a question?
Why do you choose this person?

To: Expert
9876543210 Smart Ave
World of Wisdom

There are all kinds of experts in the world.
An expert is a person who has carefully researched
and learned as much as there is to
know about something.
Somewhere in the
world, there is likely
an expert on anything
that you can think of.

Dear Expert,

Why does my tongue
sometimes stick to
Popsicles?

Answer: This happens because your tongue
is wet and the Popsicle is V-E-R-Y cold. When
your tongue touches the frozen Popsicle, the water
on your tongue freezes. The ice holds the surface of
your tongue to the surface of the Popsicle.
You should never pull
your tongue away if
it is stuck to a cold
surface. It might tear
the skin on your
tongue. Instead you
should use warm water
to melt the ice that is
holding your tongue to
the cold surface.

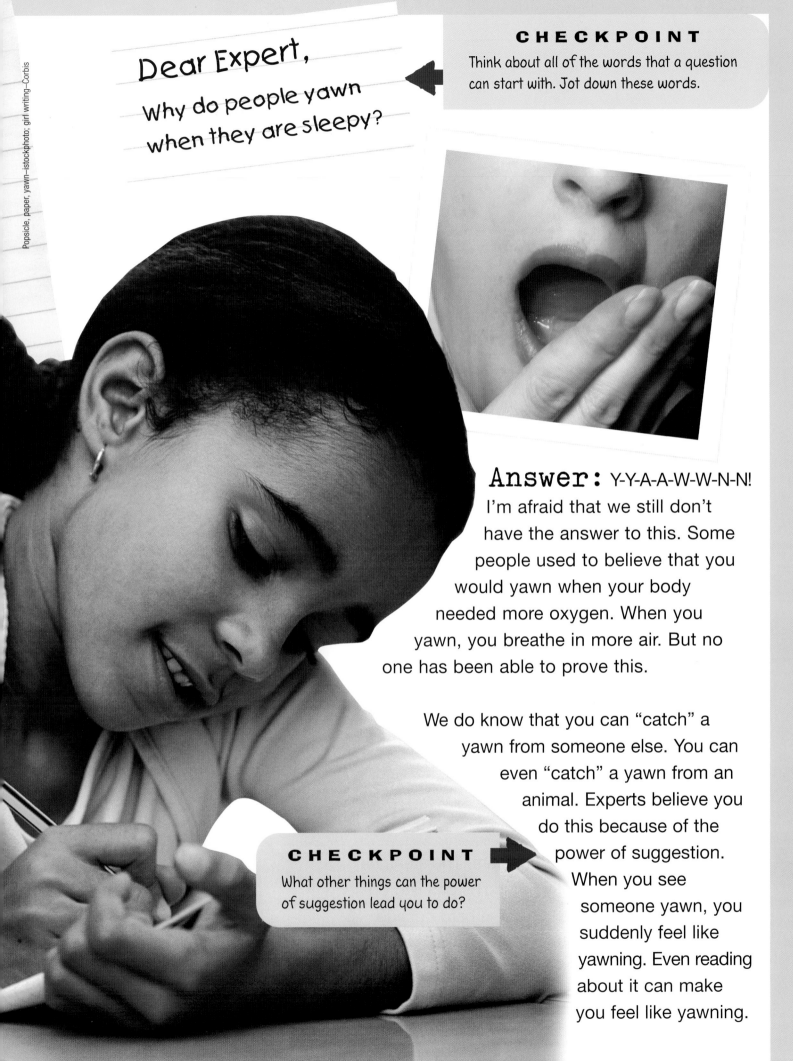

Popsicle, paper, yawn–istockphoto; girl writing–Corbis

Dear Expert,

Why do people yawn when they are sleepy?

CHECKPOINT

Think about all of the words that a question can start with. Jot down these words.

Answer: Y-Y-A-A-W-W-N-N! I'm afraid that we still don't have the answer to this. Some people used to believe that you would yawn when your body needed more oxygen. When you yawn, you breathe in more air. But no one has been able to prove this.

We do know that you can "catch" a yawn from someone else. You can even "catch" a yawn from an animal. Experts believe you do this because of the power of suggestion. When you see someone yawn, you suddenly feel like yawning. Even reading about it can make you feel like yawning.

CHECKPOINT

What other things can the power of suggestion lead you to do?

→ dust mite

Dear Expert,

Why does my mom make me vacuum under the bed if no one can see under there?

Answer:

Thousands and thousands of very small creatures called "dust mites" live under your bed. These tiny dust mites crawl around the floor feeding on the dead skin cells that are always falling from your body! Not only that, they leave behind lots and lots of droppings! The only way to see these creatures is with a microscope — but trust me, they're there! Some people are allergic to dust mite droppings. Better listen to your mom and start vacuuming! It can help to reduce the number of dust mites under your bed.

allergic: *having a negative reaction*

Dear Expert,

Why does popcorn make a popping sound when you make it?

Answer:

Inside each fresh popcorn kernel is a little bit of water. When you put the kernel in the microwave, it becomes very hot — especially on the inside. When the soft, wet part in the middle gets hot enough, it turns into a puff of steam. The steam is trapped inside the kernel so it begins pushing on the hard kernel wall. Eventually the hard outside shell bursts … POP! … to let out the steam. People who are opening a bag of microwave popcorn have to be careful not to burn themselves on the hot steam.

Dear Expert,

Why does your skin wrinkle after you have soaked in water for a long time?

Answer: After you spend a long time in water, some parts of your body, especially your feet and hands, start to look wrinkled. The outside layer of skin absorbs water, much like a sponge, and it expands. The layer of skin directly below the outside layer does not absorb as much water. So with the outside layer of skin absorbing water and expanding, the skin starts to wrinkle. The outside layer of skin is much thicker on the bottom of your feet and on your hands, so you notice the wrinkling there much more than you might on other areas of your body.

absorbs: *soaks up*

Dear Expert,

Why do pigs roll in mud?

Answer: When people are hot, their bodies begin to sweat. The sweat on their skin evaporates and cools them off. Pigs aren't able to sweat so they roll around in mud to keep cool. They also use the mud to protect their skin from the harmful effects of the sun because they can't rub on sun-block lotion like you or I can.

evaporates : *turns into vapor*

wrap up

Which question on these pages do you find most interesting and why?

WEB CONNECTIONS

Visit this website: **www.sciencemadesimple.com/science.html**. Read one of the common science questions. Test the question on a friend, as if you were an expert. Be prepared to explain the answer to your friend.

RAISING RAISINS

warm up

Looking at the title, what do you think you will read about in this story? Jot down your thoughts.

"I'm not sure what we're going to do," whined Radika to her friend Jan.

Jan and Radika were doing their homework at Radika's house and they were stuck.

"Mrs. Lee said we have to think of an experiment that shows something interesting … and we have to figure out why it happens by observing 'carefully,'" Jan reminded Radika.

"I know, I know," Radika replied, "but we have looked through loads of books and we still don't have any ideas."

"Don't worry, you'll come up with something," Radika's mom said as she walked into the bedroom. "I brought you a snack, just in case you are hungry."

Radika's mom set down a bowl filled with raisins, along with a glass of clear soda pop for each of the girls. "A special treat for my hardworking scientists," she said.

FYI

Whether they are hunting for new kinds of animals, developing new plants, or inventing new products, all scientists have two things in common — they are curious and they are careful observers.

"Wow," Radika replied, "we don't often have pop. You must really be feeling sorry for us."

Radika's mom smiled and left the room.

Radika held up the bowl of raisins for Jan. As Jan reached for some, a couple of raisins dropped into her glass of soda pop.

"Oops!" said Jan. "I guess I have raisin pop now."

"Hey!" Radika exclaimed. "Look at what's happening!"

CHECKPOINT

Using the picture as a clue, can you guess what Radika and Jan are about to observe?

Both girls looked carefully into Jan's glass of soda. One of the raisins was floating. The other one had sunk to the bottom of the glass. As they watched, the raisin on the bottom suddenly started to wobble. Then it slowly rose to the top. Meanwhile, the raisin on the top started to spin around before it dropped to the bottom.

The two raisins kept rising and falling in the glass of soda for a long time. Both girls watched what was happening very closely.

"What's going on?" asked Jan.

"I've got it figured out!" shouted Radika. "It's the bubbles in the pop!"

"What do you mean?" asked Jan.

"Well," said Radika, "Tiny bubbles from the soda pop form on the raisins. I remember Mrs. Lee teaching us that bubbles are made from trapped air. When enough bubbles have attached to the raisins, they rise to the top. As they reach the top, the bubbles pop and the raisin sinks again."

"This is a perfect experiment to bring into Mrs. Lee's class," Jan said. "This is going to be the best project we've ever done!" she added.

"You're right," replied Radika, "and we've still got lots of raisins left to eat."

FYI

Have you ever noticed the sound a can of soda pop makes when it is opened? That is the sound of gas escaping.

Soda pop has something in it that almost no other liquid has: lots of a gas called carbon dioxide. This gas was added at the soda pop factory. The minute you open a can or a bottle of soda pop, the gas starts to escape. You can see it as bubbles.

wrap up

1. In your journal, write the steps that Radika and Jan followed in their experiment.

2. Work with a partner to write about what might happen when the girls bring their homework to school the next day.

ROBOTS

Over and Over

Robots are devices or machines which are made to do the work that people might normally do. Most robots try to copy how a person or an animal might behave or act.

Over 100 years ago, a man by the name of Henry Ford came up with an idea for making lots and lots of cars. Up to that time cars were made one at a time. Mr. Ford figured out that if one worker did just one or two jobs, cars could be built in a much shorter period of time. The assembly line was born.

However, a person who made the same movements over and over again in the assembly plant often developed an injury. On top of that, the work was usually boring!

warm up

With a partner, discuss the types of work you would like a robot to do for you.

In the early 1960s, companies that made cars came up with a robot that would help with this problem. These robots could do the same job over and over again without being injured or bored.

Thinking Robots

People use their sense of sight, hearing, taste, touch and smell to learn about the world around them. Scientists have developed sensors that can give robots and machines the same type of information.

If the temperature in your house drops, the thermostat on the wall senses it and turns on the furnace. If the night light in your bedroom senses that it is dark, it switches on the light.

Today, there are small vacuum robots that can roam around your house automatically cleaning the floors and carpets. Sensors help these robots decide when and where there is work to be done. The sensors also tell the robots when they are at the edge of the stairs.

You can even buy lawnmowers that can cut grass without a human being.

These mowers use sensors to measure how high and damp the grass is and then decide how short to cut the lawn. They use solar power to move and can cut the lawn all day long if they need to.

More and more we are using robots with computer brains to do work. Sometimes robots do work that would be very dangerous for people to do, like going into space or defusing a bomb.

wrap up

1. Imagine that you could invent a robot to do anything you wanted. Create a card to introduce your robot. On the front, draw a picture of the robot. On the back, list details about it, such as:
   Name: _____
   Size: _____
   Able to do: _____

2. Sometimes when scientists invent something, it doesn't go exactly the way that they had planned. What could go wrong with a robot? Work with a partner to create a story about a robot invention that didn't work out the way it was planned.

warm up

How do you feel when you don't get enough sleep? Does it affect your school work, or how you deal with family and friends?

I magine what it would be like if you didn't have to sleep every night. You could play more games, read more books, do more homework! But not so fast, you do need to sleep.

Sound

Without enough sleep, you can become sick and even die.

You can live longer without food than you can without sleep. If you don't get enough sleep, you can become crabby or clumsy. If you don't sleep for two nights, you will become confused and have trouble doing ordinary tasks. If you don't sleep for a week, you start to imagine things. Eventually, your brain starts to shut down and is no longer able to make your body function.

CHECKPOINT

Can you remember a time when you were crabby or clumsy because you didn't have enough sleep the night before?

Why do People Need to Sleep?

Scientists still don't know all of the reasons, but many believe it is a chance for the body to rest and repair itself. People used to think that the brain shuts down at night, but we now know that isn't true. Apart from keeping all of your automatic systems going, like breathing and pumping blood, your brain is very busy when you are asleep. Dreaming is just part of the job that it is doing.

Going to Sleep

Every person has a different body clock that tells him or her when it is time to sleep. First, our brain releases a "sleepy" chemical that tells the other parts of your body that it is time to rest. You start to yawn, your muscles become heavy, your eyes start to close, and things slow down.

Step #1 Your body temperature starts to cool down. Your heart and breathing slow down, and your muscles relax.

Step #2 You are in a stage of light sleep. You can be awoken easily by a noise, smell, or touch.

Step #3 You are sound asleep. You don't feel temperature any more. Some people have frozen to death while sleeping without even waking up.

Step #4 You are in the deepest stage of sleep. Almost nothing can wake you up. This stage lasts only a few minutes at a time. During this stage, you might talk or even walk in your sleep.

Step #5 A number of times each night your brain shifts back to a stage similar to step #1. You aren't in a deep sleep but you do start dreaming. During this period your eyes flutter, which gives this part of sleep its name — REM or rapid eye movement.

By morning, you wake up rested and ready to face another day.

Dream Time

Everyone dreams, but some people remember their dreams more often than other people. Although sometimes people remember their dreams in black and white — everyone dreams in color.

FYI

- Some people will change their sleeping position more than 30 times a night.

- All living creatures go through a period when they are resting. Most people need six to ten hours of sleep each and every night. Babies sleep 16 hours a day. Bats sleep for 20 hours, and elephants sleep for only three hours a day.

A famous psychologist by the name of Sigmund Freud would analyze the dreams of his patients, hoping to find clues about how their brains were working.

You can train yourself to remember your dreams by keeping a dream diary. Here's how:

1. Put a pad of paper and a pencil next to your bed at night.

2. As you go to bed, think about something that you would like to dream about.

---

psychologist: *an expert on how the human mind works*

3. When you wake up, don't leap out of bed immediately. Lie there quietly for a couple of minutes. That way your brain can focus on what you were dreaming.

4. Write down as much of your dream as you can think of. Do it right away. The longer you wait, the less chance there is that you will remember your dream.

FYI

Robert Louis Stevenson told people that he wrote his book *The Strange Case of Dr. Jekyll and Mr. Hyde* based on nightmares that he continually had.

wrap up

1. What is the most interesting dream that you have ever had? Tell the highlights of your dream to a classmate and listen to theirs. Who gave the most detail? Who gave the least detail?

2. In one sentence, sum up how you can remember a dream.

ISAAC

By Calvin Miller

warm up

Think about this: why does an object fall to the ground when you drop it?

Sir Isaac Newton sure was smart,
beneath the apple tree.
When one fell off and hit his head,
he said, "Wow, gravity!"

For Newton was a genius
and not a common slouch.
A genius cries "Gravity!"
Most others just say "ouch!"

NEWTON

What is Gravity?

When the apple fell on his head, Newton started thinking about a certain type of motion called "gravity."

Newton knew that gravity was the force that pulled two objects together. He also knew that the larger object had the greater force (the larger object pulls the smaller object toward it). That meant that the Earth pulled smaller objects, like trees and people, toward it.

So now you know why the apple fell down instead of up. And why we stay on the ground, and do not fly into space.

wrap up

Imagine you are Isaac Newton. Tell a friend what came to your mind when the apple hit your head.

WEB CONNECTIONS

Use the Internet to find out more about gravity or Isaac Newton. Write a short report to share with your classmates.

A Weird Case of Super-Goo

Excerpt from _A Weird Case of Super-Goo_ by Kenneth Oppel

warm up

What words come to mind when you imagine a mad scientist and an experiment that goes wrong? Jot them down.

"Hey, Giles!" Aunt Lillian cried when he walked into the kitchen after school. "You're just in time!"

Just in time for what? Giles thought. The end of the world?

He felt like he'd walked into a mad scientist's laboratory.

There were four pots bubbling on the stove and something sizzling in the microwave. Things were being blended in the blender and diced and sliced in the food processor. Aunt Lillian was busy mixing something in the mixer.

The counter was buried under piles of strange herbs and spices and bottles of colored goo. And propped open everywhere were dozens of ancient herbal-recipe books, their pages splotched and stained with use.

Mom was not going to be happy when she saw all of this.

"I'm very close! Very close!" said Aunt Lillian. "And, as when cooking a good meal, timing is everything — so I'm going to need another pair of hands to do this right. Are you game?"

"Um, I'll try," said Giles.

"So. How was school?"

"I wish I was grown-up," Giles muttered.

"Why?" Aunt Lillian asked, surprised.

"I wouldn't have to go to school and have everyone laugh at my stupid hair, and I wouldn't have to see Kevin and Tina any more. I could skip all that and just get a job and go to work like Mom and Dad and every other normal adult."

"Oh, no, Giles," said Aunt Lillian. "You're not missing a thing. There are too many responsibilities when you're a grown-up. Being a kid is great. No worries! I'd trade places with you any day. All right now, roll up your sleeves. This can be messy work! I'll give you the run-down."

CHECKPOINT

Giles wants to grow up faster, and Aunt Lillian thinks being a kid is great. Who do you think is right?

She quickly led him around the kitchen, explaining what was in every pot and pan. "Alligator eyes here, cream of orchid there, that's pig's spit bubbling over there …"

KISS THE COOK

Suddenly she snatched up an old-fashioned hourglass. All the sand had settled into the bottom half.

CHECKPOINT

What is an hourglass used for?

"It's time!" she said. "Go grab those oven mitts! Ready, Giles?"

"Ready!" he yelled, above the bubbling and hissing and burbling and honking din of the kitchen.

CHECKPOINT

Listen to the sounds coming from these words.

"Let's go!"

Each gripping one end of a huge soup pot, Aunt Lillian and Giles went racing around the kitchen, grabbing saucepans and dumping the contents in all together.

"Pour!" she yelled, then, "Stir!" then, "Shake!" and then, "Stir again!" and then, "Mash!" And then, "Whisk!" she wailed, "Whisk as if your life depended on it!"

All pandemonium broke loose. The microwave was beeping, smoke was gushing from the toaster and herbs and spices were flying through the air as Aunt Lillian sprinkled them into the soup pot.

In went the green goo, then the mashed-up alligator eyes, then the goat's fingernails! The pot was quickly filling up with this strange concoction, which bubbled and splattered and gave off the most diabolical smell.

"All right! Into the oven!" cried Aunt Lillian. "Open the door, here I come!"

Giles flung open the oven door and was nearly bowled over by the blast of intense heat. She must have preheated it to a million degrees! Aunt Lillian slung the pot into the oven's bright-orange furnace mouth and slammed the door shut, panting loudly.

"Great," she said. "Excellent work, Giles. Now, in ten minutes, we'll see what we've got!"

* * * * * * * *

"Wow. They weren't kidding when they said it reduces," said Aunt Lillian, peering into the steaming pot. "Not a lot left, is there?"

Giles looked. At the bottom of the pot was a tiny slick of bluish goo. It was definitely the gooiest goo he'd ever seen. In fact, he'd have to say it was super-goo. It smelled terrible.

---

pandemonium: *confusion*

concoction: *mixture*
diabolical: *foul*
reduces: *becomes less in amount*

"Well, here goes," said Aunt Lillian, dabbing at it with her fingertip. "Ooh, still hot. Want some?"

"No, it's OK."

CHECKPOINT

What do you think Aunt Lillian will use the super-goo for?

Aunt Lillian rubbed some of the goo onto her cheek, then went back for more.

"Feels nice," she said. "I think we might have something here, Giles. I can already feel it soothing my skin. I can feel those wrinkles fading! Now, let's get some on those smile lines around the eyes. Ooooh, yes …"

She dabbed on more and more of the super-goo — until the pot was empty and her face was almost completely blue.

"Well, I feel pretty good about this, Giles. I really do."

"I don't mean to alarm you, Aunt Lillian," said Giles, "but you're beginning to glow."

"Really?" she said.

Giles nodded. It was unmistakable now —

a deep, transparent blue aura was emanating from her skin and enveloping her whole head. Aunt Lillian didn't seem terribly concerned. She walked over to a mirror to take a look.

"There's definitely a bit of a glow there," she said happily. "Of course, the books said this might happen. A healthy glow — that's all it is, Giles. I'm sure it'll fade eventually."

---

aura: *glow*
emanating: *coming from*
enveloping: *covering*

But it didn't. It got deeper and deeper and started spreading down the rest of her body over her clothing, down her neck and arms, across her chest, down towards her legs.

"Hmmm. It's a bit more powerful than I thought. But you know, Giles, I really feel younger. Do I look younger?"

CHECKPOINT

What do you think is happening to Aunt Lillian?

In fact, she was looking younger.

She was looking shorter.

She was also looking smaller! Her clothes seemed a little too big — sagging at the shoulders, bagging around the hips and ankles.

"Um, Aunt Lillian," said Giles. "I think you're shrinking."

She turned back to the mirror.

"You know, I think you're right." Her voice was different now, too — slightly higher. Her face was changing as well — smoothing out, rounding out. Her hair was sprouting and curling. And all the time, she was getting shorter and shorter. You could see it happening now, right before your eyes!

CHECKPOINT

Visualize this scene in your mind.

"It's wonderful!" Aunt Lillian cried. "I mean, look at me. I look twenty years younger … well, maybe twenty-one … or twenty-three … or twenty-four years younger …"

"Aunt Lillian?" Giles said.

Suddenly she stopped glowing, and standing before him was a girl who couldn't have been any older than him.

"Well, I think it worked," said the girl. "We've got a winner, Giles!"

At that moment, Giles heard the front door open.

"Hello!" Mrs. Barnes called out.

Mrs. Barnes walked into the kitchen and stopped dead in her tracks, staring at the colossal mess.

CHECKPOINT

Mrs. Barnes is Giles's mother and Lillian's sister.

"What on Earth have you been doing?" she demanded.

"Just a little experiment, Liz," said Lillian.

---

colossal: *huge*

Both Aunt Lillian and Giles were standing very still, watching Mrs. Barnes, waiting for her reaction. But she was too busy taking in the dirty pots and pans, the seeping mess on the counters, the gooey footprints across the tiles.

"Well, you can start cleaning it up right now, both of you. I knew this would happen, Lillian, with all this hocus pocus you … you were …"

Mrs. Barnes's gaze now settled on her younger sister, and on the over-sized clothes hanging from her small body. A frown of confusion flickered across her brow.

"Lillian?" she said. "What happened to your clothes? They're huge!" said Mrs. Barnes.

"What are you doing in clothes so … big, so …"

Mrs. Barnes took a quick step back, her eyes wide. "Lillian, you're … small!"

"I'm young," she said happily.

"About eleven, I figure," said Giles.

Mrs. Barnes narrowed her eyes suspiciously. "All right, what's going on here? What have you done?"

"It's the super-goo," sighed Giles.

"My wrinkle cream," Aunt Lillian explained. "It worked!"

"A little too well," Giles added.

"It turned you back into an eleven-year-old?" Mrs. Barnes said in a dazed voice. "All those herbs and spices and crackpot recipes?"

"Wonderful, isn't it?"

"No, it is not wonderful!" roared Mrs. Barnes. "I spent my whole childhood taking care of you, little sister, and I am not prepared to do it again! Now, I want you to just … grow up, this minute!"

"That might be a bit of a problem."

"Why?"

---

suspiciously: *distrustfully*

"Well, first of all, I think the wrinkle cream might be permanent. And second of all, I don't want to grow up."

CHECKPOINT

Why would Aunt Lillian not want to be an adult again?

"What do you mean, you don't want to? You're eleven years old! You're telling me you want to stay this way?"

"Yes. How many people get the chance to have their youth again, Liz? I'm not going to miss out on a chance like this!"

"Oh no," said Mrs. Barnes. "Not on your life. You are not staying young, Lillian. Absolutely not."

Aunt Lillian just smiled stubbornly. "Oh, yes, I am."

wrap up

1. What did the super-goo do to Aunt Lillian? List the changes that happened to her.

2. Imagine you are Giles or Aunt Lillian. Write a journal entry to explain how you felt.

ACKNOWLEDGMENTS

The publisher gratefully acknowledges the following for permission to reprint copyrighted material in this book.

Every reasonable effort has been made to trace the owners of copyrighted material and to make due acknowledgment. Any errors or omissions drawn to our attention will be gladly rectified in future editions.

Calvin Miller: "Isaac Newton." From *Apples, Snakes and Bellyaches*, copyright © 1993, reprinted by permission of the author.

"The Perfect Igloo" from *Nestor's Dock* by Tom Labaff. Reprinted by permission of Cricket Magazine Group, Carus Publishing Company from *ASK* magazine February 2004, Vol. 3, No. 2, © 2004 by Carus Publishing Company.

"A Weird Case of Super-Goo" excerpt from *Weird Case of Super-Goo*, copyright © 1996, 2002 by Kenneth Oppel, reprinted by permission of Scholastic Canada Ltd.

Play-Doh: © 2003-2005 Hasbro. All rights reserved.